COMMON
THOUGHTS
FOR AN
UNCOMMON
FEAST

COMMON THOUGHTS FOR AN UNCOMMON FEAST

JANICE V. BAILEY

ARPress

ILLUMINATING IDEAS
EMPOWERING VOICES

ARPress
45 Dan Road Suite 5
Canton, MA 02021

Hotline: 1(888) 821-0229
Fax: 1(508) 545-7580

Ordering Information:
Quantity sales. Special discounts are available on quantity purchases by corporations, associations, and others. For details, contact the publisher at the address above.

Printed in the United States of America.

ISBN-13:	Softcover	979-8-89330-334-6
	eBook	979-8-89330-335-3
	Hardback	979-8-89330-347-6

Library of Congress Control Number: 2024900488

CONTENTS

I dedicate this book to my husband of forty-four years. Though it is a small gift with simple thoughts about the communion meal, it is inspired by Randy, who is my inspiration.

Acts 2:42 (KJV): And they continued steadfastly in the apostles' doctrine, fellowship, in the breaking of bread, and in prayer.

WHAT IF?

What if Moses had just glanced at the burning bush and not investigated any further? He would have missed the opportunity of speaking to God. He would have missed the opportunity of being a great leader of God's people. When Peter was on the rooftop, what if he had been too deep in thought and prayer to notice the sheet coming down from heaven with all the animals on it? If that hadn't happened, who would have convinced the other apostles that even the Samaritans, the heathens, and the Gentiles were allowed the same opportunities for salvation as the Jewish people? What if Judas hadn't betrayed Jesus? We could ask "what if?" all day.

We have heard the expression "living in the moment." It is great to make plans for tomorrow, to plan for the future, but it is also important to be in the moment that you are in now.

Jesus was asked, "What is the greatest commandment?" He replied, "To love the Lord your God with all your heart, soul and mind, and to love your neighbor as yourself." Jesus spoke so often in parables, but it isn't hard to understand what He meant when as He took the bread and broke it, He said, "This is my body given for you; do this in remembrance of me." The same way He took the cup, saying, "This cup is the new covenant in my blood; do this and whenever you drink it, in remembrance of me." The apostle Paul also said, "A man ought to examine himself before he eats the bread and drinks the cup."

So now I ask, "Are you living in the moment?" If we aren't focusing on the significance of these emblems, then where are we?

> 1For I received from the Lord what I also pass on to you. The Lord Jesus on the night he was betrayed, took bread, and when he had given thanks, he broke it and said, "This is my body, which is for you, do this in remembrance of me." In the same way, after supper, he took the cup saying, "This is the new covenant in my blood; do this whenever you drink it in remembrance of me."
>
> - 1 Corinthians 11:23-25

Our Heart

An average heart weighs about 11 to 12 ounces. Your heart beats at the average rate of 100,000 to 115,000 times a day. Each day, a heart pumps approximately 2,000 gallons of blood through our bodies. A healthy heart can do amazing things. If our hearts stop, we will die. I am obviously speaking about the physical heart, which is the most important muscle in our bodies that sustains our physical lives.

As Christians, we also have a spiritual heart. In God's Word, the word "heart" represents the center of our emotions, our thinking, and our reasoning. We could call it the command center of our lives.

In life, there will always be demands upon our time and energy or things that need our attention. However, the most urgent of needs is for us to have our hearts aligned with God's will. Therefore, when Jesus tells us to, "Do this in remembrance of me," I believe that it is important. It is the most significant time in our worship service. Because around this table, we are powerfully reminded just how much God loves us, giving us another chance to renew our pledge, promise, and covenant we have with the **One** who saved us.

> Psalm 51:10 (NKJV): Create in me a pure heart. Oh God, and renew a right spirit within me.

Nothing Hidden

God chose David as king over His people. David was a king after God's own heart. God was pleased with David until his sins of adultery and murder alienated him from God. You and I know it isn't possible to hide from God. It wasn't until Nathan the prophet confronted David with his sins that David repented and asked God for His forgiveness. His sins were not hidden like he thought.

We are a lot like David in this respect. We may not repent until someone confronts us about our sin. Our sin may be hidden from the world, yet it is always visible to God.

I hope that we might have the mindset like David when he asked God to create in him a clean heart and to renew a right spirit unto him.

This is a perfect time to examine ourselves as we consider the life we led this past week.

Meeting around this table can help us to focus on the blood that flowed down Golgotha's hill as the perfect Son of God was sacrificed for each of us.

John 3:16: For God so loved the world, that he gave his only begotten son, that whosoever believed in him, shall not perish but have eternal life.

Matthew 10:28 (NKJV): Do not fear those who can kill the body, but cannot kill the soul. But, rather fear him who is able to destroy both body and soul in hell.

Disaster or Crisis

None of us will ever forget 9/11. There have been numerous disasters and crises we will never forget. I am sure we each have crises and disasters in our own lives that have brought us to our knees.

We can get very disheartened and discouraged when listening to our daily news. It is worldwide that we hear of tornadoes, hurricanes, mudslides, and homes and towns being destroyed. If that's not enough, we have school shootings and murder and violence daily. It's on a positive note, however, where the compassion of people shines forth, such as first responders, people with donations, free counseling, people standing in line to donate blood, etc. There is an ongoing crisis that plagues the world today. It is a spiritual crisis. People all over the world need the Lord Jesus Christ.

Christians are not immune and will become victims of disasters and trouble. But there is hope for us. Apostle Paul told us that we are more than conquerors.

For brothers and sisters who meet around this communion table, we recognize and contemplate the significance of these emblems. We celebrate the One who didn't just donate pints of His blood; He sacrificed all His blood that we might live eternally with Him.

Psalm 103:10-13: He does not treat us as our sins deserve or repay us according to our iniquities. For as high as the heavens are above the earth, so great is his love for those who fear him; as far as the east is from the west, so far has he removed our transgressions from us.

Hebrews 8:12 (KJV): For I will forgive their wickedness and will remember their sin no more.

UNREMEMBERED

I read a book titled Unremembered. The story is about a plane crash over the ocean where all passengers and crew were lost with the exception of a young sixteen-year-old girl. The rescue team found her body floating in the water among the wreckage. Miraculously, she was unharmed, but she suffered severe amnesia. She had no memory of her past. Her memories began at the time of her rescue.

The story reminded me of how blessed we are. Even though we didn't witness the life, death, or resurrection of Christ, we have detailed accounts from several eyewitnesses who recorded the same events.

Unlike the girl in the book, it might be a good thing that we can remember our pasts, as they can be reminders of the wonderful grace and mercy God has shown us when we become obedient to His gospel. Our ways are not God's ways, and our thoughts are not God's thoughts. Our hearts can rejoice when we read these scriptures.

Such comforting thoughts—as we meet around this table, we are proclaiming the Lord's death and His resurrection as we anxiously await His return.

> John 3:16 (NIV): For God so loved the world that he gave his one and only son; that whosoever believes in him, shall not perish, but have eternal life.

Romans 5:6-8 (NIV): You see at just the right time, while we were still powerless, Christ died for the ungodly. Very rarely will anyone die for a righteous man, though for a good man someone might possibly dare to die. But God demonstrates his own love for us in this: While we were still sinners, Christ died for us.

Too Good to Be True

We all have heard the expression, "If it sounds too good to be true, then it probably is."

I recently read about a businessman who did all his work with his computer from his home. He was constantly getting emails with offers where he could make as much as $25,000 a week. He had even gotten emails stating he might have free money waiting for him if he contacted the company (or individual) within twenty-four hours. All these offers sounded "too good to be true."

Curiosity got the best of him. He totaled up what he would receive if he took all these emails at face value; his monies would be over $250,000! Wow, that sounded great! Of course, these offers were from scam artists. As long as we live, we will be faced with people telling and selling lies.

However, there is one offer that might sound too good to be true, but it is true. As a matter of fact, it was a stumbling block to the Jewish people. The offer is found throughout the New Testament.

We come around this table to celebrate the Lord's death and His return. To the world, this may sound too good to be true, but to believers, it is a powerful truth.

John 3:3 (NIV): I tell you the truth, no one can see the kingdom of God unless he is born again.

WHO CAN BE SAVED?

In John chapter 8 is recorded the story where Jesus went early one morning to teach the people who gathered around Him. The Pharisees and the teachers of the law brought to him a woman in the act of adultery. They placed her in the middle of the crowd and said to Jesus, "Teacher, this woman was caught in act of adultery, and in the law, Moses commanded us to stone such women. Now what do you say?" We know they were trying to trap Jesus so they might have a reason to accuse Him.

Jesus responded by stooping down and began writing in the dirt with His finger. There has been a lot of speculation as to what Jesus was writing. Was Jesus writing down the sins of the men who wanted to stone her? Some have said that Jesus was drawing in the dirt as He waited for His response to sink into the minds of those gathered there. One artist portrayed Jesus drawing a cross in the dirt, foreshadowing of His death.

Jesus said, "If any among you is without sin, let him cast the first stone." It is written that the crowd threw down the stones and left. Jesus told the adulteress outcast that He didn't condemn her and to go and sin no more—a beautiful story of forgiveness.

You and I were outcasts. However, since we have believed and obeyed the gospel, we can be assured that all Jesus's promises are for us.

When we meet around the table, recognizing the emblems as Christ shed His blood and broken body, we are keeping our covenant with Him. Listen closely: I can imagine Jesus saying, "Neither do I condemn you, go and sin no more." "A man ought to examine himself before he eats of the bread and drinks of the cup" (1 Cor. 11:28).

CLEAN OR NOT CLEAN

We have a granddaughter who has an odd way of cleaning her room. She will gather all her clothes, dirty or not, and put them in one basket for dirty laundry. She then proceeds to shove everything within sight into her closet and shuts the door. As far as she is concerned, as long as you can see the floor and walk into the room without stepping on things, the room is clean. Sometimes I think we behave this way too. We may have secret thoughts or hidden faults that aren't visible to the eye. We may look and act wholesome and good. On the outside, we may appear to be wonderful Christians. Our cups (our bodies) on the outside appear clean, but on the inside, we are still dirty. In the book of Romans, Paul told us that while we were still sinners, Christ died for us. That is a tremendously powerful statement.

We have an excellent opportunity as we meet around this table to clean our cups, confessing and repenting of our sins and shortcomings as we also recognize these emblems of the perfect, sacrificial Son of God.

Like the song says, there is power in the blood.

> Hebrews 10:25 (NIV): Do not forsake the assembly as some are in the habit of doing.
>
> 1 Corinthians 10:15-16 (NIV): I speak to sensible people; judge for yourselves what I say, "Is it not the cup of thanksgiving for

which we give thanks, a participation of the blood of Christ? And is it not the bread we break a participation in the body of Christ?"

ROUTINE BECOMES HABIT

Routines…we all have them. You may drink a cup of coffee the first thing in the morning. Maybe you always read the newspaper as you eat your breakfast. Perhaps you rise early to exercise before going to work. Do you have a routine time that you devote to reading God's Word? I've heard it said that if we do something for thirty straight days, it becomes a habit. The thing about routines and habits are they can be good or they can be bad. We do things like brushing **our teeth regularly or having our routine check- ups for good reasons.**

A friend once told me that her congregation doesn't participate (I prefer the term celebrate) in the communion service, except for Christmas and Easter. They didn't want communion to become too routine or a habit, so twice a year was sufficient. She mentioned that by doing it twice a year, they would become excited as they anticipated these two services.

As a Christian, I am of the mindset that some habits are "good and necessary." Would our lives be different if we didn't have our check-ups or watch our diets, not brushing our teeth daily or practicing good hygiene? The answer is yes.

I admit it does take a concentrated effort sometimes to focus on what the communion service is about. But, isn't it true that Jesus told us to do this? As often as we do this, do it in remembrance of Him. This is how we do it; we meet together routinely and habitually so we won't forget. This table before us is part of our spiritual check-up.

Hebrews 10:25 (NIV): Do not forsake the assembly as some are in the habit of doing.

ATTITUDE

When my children were small, we taught them a song that has the chorus saying, "He's still working on me...to make me what I ought to be."

A man named Pablo Casals was considered one of the most gifted cello players of the twentieth century. According to a story, a young reporter asked Pablo, "Mr. Casals, you are ninety-five years old and the greatest cello player that has ever lived, so why do you still practice six hours a day?" Pablo replied, "Because I think I'm making progress." What a great attitude.

As Christians, we should never be satisfied with our growth in knowledge of the Word or our spiritual growth. We won't reach our pinnacle of spiritual success until we see Jesus face to face. When Jesus said, "I am the vine, you are the branches. He who abides in me, and I in him, bears much fruit," that is a wonderful promise. Jesus told His disciples that if they loved Him, they would obey all the things He commanded. We should follow the same path that Christ and His apostles did. We should follow the example Christ instituted at the last meal He shared with His friends. He took bread and broke it, giving it to the apostles and said, "Take eat, this is my body." And He also took the cup and passed it and proclaimed, "This is the new covenant in my blood. Do this, whenever you drink it, in remembrance of me."

Around the table, we reflect and remember the great gift and hope of our salvation.

> 2 Corinthians 4:16 (NIV): Therefore we do not lose heart. Though outwardly we are wasting away, yet inwardly we are being renewed day by day.

RESTORATION

Two artistic masterpieces by Leonardo Da Vinci, as well as many others, have skillfully been restored and preserved. It is a wonderful thing that techniques have been developed to restore such masterpieces and works of art.

I am reminded of the message Paul gave to the people of Corinth; the message was about the restoration of mankind. Paul wrote, "You have put off the old man with his deeds and have put on the new man who is renewed or restored in knowledge according to the image of him who created him." God is not attempting to renovate the work of a deceased artist. It is a spiritual renewal from the living God, who created us and now gives us new lives in His Son, Jesus Christ. His forgiveness relieves our burden of sin, and His grace continually covers our shortcomings. It doesn't matter how damaged we may be; there is always hope for renewal and restoration for you and me.

When we meet around this table each week, it is a reminder of how far God is willing to go to restore us back to Himself. Coming together around this communion meal is our response to Christ's word when He spoke to His apostles: "Take eat, this is my body that was broken for you. Do this is remembrance of me."

Romans 5:7-8: Very rarely will anyone die for a righteous man; though for a good man, someone might possibly die. But, God demonstrates his love for us in this; which while we were still sinners, Christ died for us.

Just As I Am

In the real estate business, you find homes for sale by the owner. They sell the house, **"Just as is."** Usually this means that the owner knows that repairs and renovations are needed. If you want it, you must take it just as it is.

Forty-three years ago, our family began growing, and we needed space for our three children. We had agents take us all over the area, looking for a suitable home. There was nothing on the market within our price range or what we desired. That was a long time ago, and we have raised three children and grandchildren, and we are still in the same house we wanted to move out of. We decided to take the home we had as is, you could say, and built the extra rooms we needed for our family.

Jesus tells us to come to Him just as we are. He accepts us with all our flaws and imperfections. He does the fixing and repairing through the Holy Spirit.

Though we are sinners, we are saved by God's wonderful grace. We meet around this table each Sunday to celebrate His death and resurrection.

Romans 8:1 (NIV): Therefore, there is no condemnation for those who are in Christ Jesus.

Hebrews 4:16 (NIV): Let us therefore come boldly before the throne of grace, that we may obtain mercy and find grace.

No Fear

The Israelites in the Old Testament could not approach God without fear. When God thundered on Mount Sinai, the people trembled. They were so afraid of God that they wanted Moses to speak to God on their behalf. Later, when access to God was granted to the Levite priests, they had to follow very specific instructions (Lev. 16:1-34).

Christians today can approach God without fear; this is such an awesome blessing. This is made possible through Jesus's death and resurrection. The result of Christ's sacrificial death on our behalf is that God's penalty for our sin has been satisfied.

Because of our Savior Jesus Christ, we can approach God anytime or anywhere. We have instant access.

Around this table, we are in God's presence. We can bring our repentant hearts and our praise. We do this with grateful hearts and not fearful hearts.

> John 15:5 (CSB): I am the vine, you are the branches, the one who remains in me and I in him produces much fruit, because you can do nothing without me.

INDEPENDENCE

Each year, we celebrate Independence Day on July 4th. In the beginning, there were only thirteen colonies. Independence is great. Many people have a goal of becoming independently wealthy. Senior citizens want to maintain their independence in their late years. Teenagers talk about gaining their independence from the parents. Physical, personal, or financial independence is something for which we strive for.

What about our spiritual lives? Can we really be independent where our spiritual wellness is concerned?

We will fail if we do not remain in Christ. How we remain or abide in Christ is: A) staying in the Word of God; B) staying in fellowship with believers; C) staying strong and diligent in our prayer lives; D) obeying what we read in Scripture and loving mankind.

We are far from being self-reliant spiritually. We are totally dependent on the One who died to set us free. Every day can be our "Dependent Day."

Psalm 103:12 (CSB): As far as the East is from the West so far, he has removed our transgressions from us.

Philippians 3:13-14 (CSB): But one thing I do. Forgetting what is behind, and reaching forward to what is ahead.

DON'T BE HAUNTED

A story has been told of two men who gave their lives to Christ while they were incarcerated. The younger man was very discouraged because the family from which he had robbed would not forgive him. The older prisoner said, "My crime was so violent, it continues to haunt and affect a family to this day. They have not forgiven me because their pain is so great. At first, I found myself longing for their forgiveness." He continued his story, "Then one day I realized I was being selfish, I was thinking only of myself and how bad I felt. It's a lot for that family to forgive me. I was focused on what I felt and thought I needed, which was their forgiveness before I could heal. It took some time to realize that their forgiveness of me was a matter between them and God." The younger man asked him, "How can you stand it?" The older man explained, "What God did for him, something he didn't deserve when Christ died for his sins." God keeps His promise to remove my sin as far as the east is from the west. He also promised that He will not remember my sins (Isa. 43:25).

We show God honor when we accept and believe in His love and His sacrifice. His love and forgiveness are sufficient for us. We must forget what lies behind.

Around this table, we begin a new day, a new beginning. We have this time to evaluate our lives from this past week and press on to become more like Christ.

It is by His blood we are cleansed.

> Luke 5:16 (CSB): But Jesus often withdrew to lonely places and prayed.

Turn It Off

A family took a trip to Northern Wisconsin to visit their grandparents. The grandparents lived in a mountainous region and didn't have good television reception. The grandfather watched his grandson fiddle around with the television for a while. After about thirty minutes into his trying, the grandson turned to his grandfather in frustration and said, "What do you do if you get only one channel and you don't like what's on that channel?" The grandfather smiled at the young boy and said, "Try turning it off." This really wasn't the response his grandson wanted.

We have so many things in today's world to distract, entertain, and inform us. Between television, iPhones, and computers, we can really become too addicted and connected to technology. Sometimes we do need to just turn it off and unplug ourselves from the things that seem to dominate our time and energy.

Jesus often withdrew Himself at times—especially when He wanted time to pray (Matt. 14:13). He encouraged His disciples to step away even for just a brief time (Mark 6:31). The time for solitude and reflection is not just beneficial for us—it is necessary. It's in these moments we find it easier to draw nearer to God. It is good for our bodies, minds, and spirits.

Turning down the volume of things that distract us allows us to listen and hear God more effectively. Around this table is a perfect opportunity to unplug our minds from the world outside as we draw near to the heart of God.

1 Corinthians 1:18 (CSB): For the message of the cross is foolishness to those who are perishing, but to those of us who are being saved, it is the power of God.

HANDLE WITH CARE

W hen our children were first born, I was very hesitant to hold them. They seemed so tiny and fragile. I thought the phrase "Fragile: handle with care" should be stamped on them somewhere. I was nervous when friends and family came around to visit the new addition to the family. I held my breath as I watched everyone passing my precious child around from person to person with such ease. I never said it aloud, but I was thinking, *Be careful; handle her gently.*

By the time our third child was born, I was more comfortable, of course. I am a grandparent now, but I still think babies are fragile and need to be handled with care.

I was thinking about the gospel, the message of Christ. We need to handle it with care. It isn't fragile; however, it is quite powerful. It is able to do a heart transplant without cutting into the human body.

When we come together around this table in participation of the communion meal, we do it because Christ told us to. A very important thought as we eat this bread and drink this cup is…we must handle it with care. By this I mean we should recognize His birth, His life, His sacrifice, and His return. He is worthy of our thoughts and our praise, so our hearts and minds should be focused on Him. Let us handle with care the Lord's Supper.

1 Corinthians 11:27-28: So then, whoever eats the bread and drinks the cup of the Lord in an unworthy manner will be guilty of sin against the body and the blood of the Lord. Let a person examine himself; in this way let him eat of the bread and drink of the cup.

YOUR REFLECTION

Have you ever seen your reflection in a pool of water? In 1835, a German chemist named Justus von Liebig developed a process for applying a thin layer of metallic silver to one side of a pane of glass. You and I use his invention daily. Of course, I am talking about the mirror. Now we don't have to find a lake or puddle of water to see our reflection. Then came the invention of the camera. We now can take our fascination about how we look to a new level. Skip ahead a few decades, and we have cellphones with a camera. It is so easy to lose count of all the selfies that are taken daily.

One of the troubles in our society is that we tend to focus more on our outward appearances than ever before. We would be better off if we spent more time focusing on our inner selves. The Word of God tells us mankind looks on the outward appearance, but God looks at our hearts. James, Jesus's brother, told us to look into the mirror of God's Word so we can see ourselves more clearly. Self -examination is crucial for a healthy spiritual life. God wants us to really see ourselves so if there is sin, we can turn from it. The point of self-examination is to make ourselves right with God.

My hope is that we are more concerned with the reflection of our hearts toward God than we are thinking about what we look like in a mirror.

For as often as you eat this bread and drink this cup, you do show the Lord's death till he comes. Wherefore, whosoever shall eat this bread and drink the cup of the Lord, unworthily, shall be guilty of the body and blood of the Lord. But let a man examine himself. Let him eat of that bread and drink of the cup. For he that eateth and drinketh unworthily, eateth and drinketh damnation to himself, not discerning the Lord's body.

- 1 Corinthians 11:26-30 (NIV)

GOOD VERSUS GREAT

A young man was distracted by the sunlight streaming through the church windows. His eyes were drawn in fascination to the sunrays dancing and moving across the faces of the people in the pews. His mind stopped focusing on the words from the pulpit. He was listening to the sweet sound of the birds chirping and singing outside. He noticed that somewhere close to the church, a person had chosen to mow his or her lawn. Between the sunlight shining through the windows, the birds singing, and the sound of grass being mowed, he had a difficult time focusing during the worship service.

This reminds me of the story of Mary and Martha. Mary sat at the feet of Jesus, while Martha was preoccupied and frustrated about the meal she was preparing for Jesus and the guests. Martha was being hospitable, while Mary was being transformed by her Savior.

Have you heard the expression, "Good things can become enemies of great things"?

Is anything distracting you today? Jesus would not have said it if it wasn't important to Him.

> 2 Corinthians 4:16 (NIV): Therefore, do not lose heart. Though outwardly we are wasting away, yet inwardly we are being renewed daily.

Are You Being Renewed?

Do you know how many stars are in the atmosphere? My seven-year-old grandson tells me there are a bazillion! Well, we can try to count or guess forever, but God not only knows how many He created, He also calls them by name.

In the book of Genesis, we read that God created the heavens and the earth and all things in them. He also knows the number of hairs on each of our heads. He knows about our failures and our triumphs.

The moment we obeyed the gospel message, we became children of God. We belong to the God who sent His only Son to be sacrificed in order that we might be saved. The knowledge of what Christ did for us can't ever be overstated.

A British author, J.B. Phillips, called the earth "the visited planet, where the prince of glory is busy working out his plan."

Jesus calls us to this table to remember the death and the resurrection of His sacrificed body. We meet to renew our hope in His return.

> Jesus said, "I am the living bread which came down from heaven: if any man eat of this bread, he shall live forever; the bread that I will give is my flesh, which I shall give for the life of the world. The Jews therefore talked among themselves, saying, "how can this man give us his flesh to eat?" Then Jesus said to them, "Verily,

verily I say unto you. Except ye eat the flesh of the Son of man, and drink his blood, ye have no life in you. Whosoever eateth my flesh, and drinketh my blood, hath eternal life and I will raise him up at the last day."

- John 6:51-57

A RIDDLE

What is greater than God and more evil than Satan? The poor have it, the rich need it, and if you eat it, you will die. The answer is **nothing**.

Sometimes we find ourselves in the middle of a crisis. Worries and troubles seem to besiege us every day. The details of our daily ordeals can so easily distract us from God.

Whether you are rich or poor, we all are needy. We need a Savior.

What we do around this table each week is our response to Jesus. This table is part of His plan.

> Romans 7:15-16 (CSB): For I do not understand what I am doing. Because I do not practice what I want to do, but I do what I hate.

What I Do

Have you ever caught yourself thinking, *Now, why did I do that?* or *Wish I hadn't done that!?*

The apostle Paul had this same affliction. Paul said, "I find myself doing things I don't want to do, and not doing the things I want to do."

If the apostle Paul had problems with his behavior and actions, then certainly we aren't exempt from bad behavior.

A few years ago, a popular item was a rubber or fabric bracelet that had WWJD on it. The letters stood for "What Would Jesus Do?" The idea behind the bracelet was to remind us to do what Jesus would do in any situation.

Always trying to respond as Jesus would is a wonderful attitude. The Roman cross speaks volumes; this communion meal before us speaks even more. We remember what Jesus did to redeem us and reconcile us back to God.

Amazing love, how can it be that the Son of God would die for me?

> 1 Corinthians 11:28: Let a person examine himself; in this way let him eat the bread and drink from the cup. For whoever eats and drinks without recognizing the body, eats and drinks judgement on himself.

DISTRACTION CAN LEAD TO DISASTER

Have you ever seen someone driving a vehicle while trying to text on his or her phone? I have, on a daily basis. I have also seen folks talking on the phone, putting on make-up, trying to eat, trying to look at a map while driving, etc. They know they should be focused on their driving but continue to do these things. Distracted driving is very dangerous.

I'm sure you remember the story of Mary and Martha. Jesus was concerned about Martha. She was so distracted by all the preparation to be made for the meal she was going to serve. Martha complained to Jesus about Mary not assisting her in the preparing of the meal. Jesus said, "Martha, Martha, you are worried and troubled about many things. But one thing is needed, and Mary has chosen the good part. Which will not be taken away from her."

Christ, in His wisdom, set the example for us to meet around the communion table. We should not become distracted by the world but should focus on the One who created the world. Partaking in this meal is like our pledge of allegiance to Christ.

Hebrews 10:25 (CSB): Do not give up meeting together, as some are in the habit of doing, but encourage one another-and all the more as you see the day approaching.

DON'T FORGET

We have a large calendar hanging on our kitchen wall. The calendar is written all over as we have marked birthdays, anniversaries, appointments, and events happening each month. I find myself looking at the calendar several times a day to remind myself of what is on the schedule. If I hadn't marked the calendar, I certainly would forget.

It must be human nature for us to be forgetful. The Israelites seemed to have forgotten how God had provided for them as they traveled through the wilderness all those years. They began complaining about everything.

In God's infinite wisdom and because we are a forgetful people, God gave us a simple plan to help us remember His sacrifice for our sin. This table consists of bread and the fruit of the vine. It serves as a powerful reminder of His broken body and shed blood. Take this in remembrance of Christ.

> Psalm 16:5-6 (CSB): Lord you are my portion and my cup of blessing, you hold my future. The boundary lines have fallen for me in pleasant places; indeed I have a beautiful inheritance.

THANKFUL DRUG

During my meditation recently, my heart and mind became overwhelmed with sadness. Daily, people are experiencing anxiety and fear, but their reaction to these emotions is troubling. Hatred and violence will never make us feel better. Actually, these are two of Satan's tools. It is heartbreaking to see how society is responding to the circumstances our world is facing right now.

Scientists and chemists work tirelessly trying to create a drug or vaccine to help us fight the coronavirus COVID-19. But a vaccine will not help hatred or fear.

A prominent researcher at Duke University Medical Center said, "If **thankfulness** were a drug, it would be the world's best-selling product with health benefits for every organ in our body."

Thankfulness is simply living with a sense of gratitude, recognizing and focusing on the things we have instead of things we wish we had. Scripture takes the idea to a deeper level. The act of giving thanks makes us think of our blessings but also the One who gives us the blessings.

Meeting around this communion table can help calm our minds and soothe our souls. This is a quiet place with Jesus. We can renew our hope for lives in eternity, regardless of what is going in our world. Let us focus on our Lord with thankful hearts.

1 Corinthians 11:28 (CSB): Let a man examine himself, then, eat the bread and drink of the cup.

MAINTENANCE

father was teaching his fifteen-year-old son how to drive. While instructing him, he took the opportunity to also teach him about basic automobile maintenance. He took him the local service station, where he showed his son how to check the oil level while they filled up with gas. The father told him that it would be good maintenance if he would check the oil each time he filled the tank with gas. When the son was grown and owned his own automobile, he said that each time he filled up with gasoline, he would remember what his dad taught him as he quoted the slogan, "Oil is cheap; engines are expensive. Adding a quart of oil is nothing compared to replacing an engine."

I think we all believe that it's important to keep up good maintenance on our vehicles. It is also very important that we practice good maintenance in our spiritual lives. David prayed in Psalm 5:3, "In the morning Lord, you hear my voice. In the morning Lord, I plead my case to you, and watch expectantly." David talked to God each morning. Some of us prefer prayer and reading the Word upon rising, while some may prefer the evening. The important thing is that we do spend personal time with God. Consider it basic spiritual maintenance. It isn't magic—it takes effort, but it will help us maintain a personal relationship with God.

The opportunity we have to meet around the communion table each week helps us to remain steadfast in our commitment and covenant with Christ.

We meet to celebrate Christ in discerning His broken body and spilled blood for our sins.

Isaiah 53:5 (NIV): But he was wounded for our transgressions; he was crushed for our iniquities; upon him was the chastisement that brought us peace, and with stripes we are healed.

Are You Cleansed?

Our Scripture text is found in Luke 17:11-19. Jesus was on His way to Jerusalem as He traveled the border between Samaria and Galilee. This is where He encountered ten men with leprosy. The men cried out to Jesus in a loud voice, "Jesus, master, have pity on us!" When Jesus saw them, He said, "Go show yourselves to the priests." As they went, they were cleansed. One of them, when he saw he was healed, came back, praising God in a loud voice. He threw himself at Jesus's feet and thanked Him, and he was a Samaritan. Jesus said, "Were there not ten cleansed? Where are the other nine? Was no one found to return and give praise to God except this foreigner?" Then Jesus said to the Samaritan, "Rise, your faith has made you well."

My thought when I read this passage are, why did only one of the lepers return to Jesus? He came back with thankfulness and gratitude toward Jesus for his physical healing. Yet, Jesus responded to him about his faith making him well. Jesus had given him a spiritual healing, something much greater than a healing from leprosy.

You and I meet around this communion table because of our faith. We believe Jesus when He says that these emblems are His body and blood. We believe Paul when he said that faith is our victory. Listen closely: can you hear in the silence Jesus saying, "Eat and drink of this meal, your faith has made you well"?

John 4:24 (NAS): God calls us to worship in spirit and truth.

ARE YOU PREPARED?

We have a Christian service camp in our area. It has proven to be a catalyst for a lot of young people who go into the ministry.

My fifteen-year-old granddaughter spent several weeks during the summer not only as a camper but serving as a counselor for younger children.

I enjoyed her enthusiasm as she told me about all the things that happened at the camp. I would watch her pack, unpack, and repack her suitcase as she prepared for another week of camp. She reminded me of how important it is to be prepared for today, tomorrow, and this week ahead. If you want to develop a good habit, then preparedness would be a great one.

I wonder, how prepared are we for this week? Are we enthusiastic for the opportunities that will come our way? Are we excited that we may get the chance to share the gospel? Are we enthused about meeting around this table with the Lord? Jesus said, "As often as ye do this, you show the Lord's death until he comes." Are we prepared for His return?

Acts 2:42: They devoted themselves to the apostles teaching, to fellowship, to the breaking of bread and prayer.

FORGOTTEN MEMORIES

My niece recently sent a family picture that was taken many years ago. It was the last photo of my parents together with the whole family. Looking at the photo, I recall how difficult it was to get the entire family together in one place. I hadn't thought about that day for many years. The memory isn't really forgotten; it is still in the recesses of my mind. It just took that one picture to spark the memory and events of that day.

God created us, and He definitely knows how our minds work. Perhaps that is the reason Jesus tells us many times to meet around this communion table. How often do we meditate on the cross or contemplate the empty grave?

A bloody cross and an empty grave—what should they bring to our minds? Just like the family portrait reminded me of the day it was taken, these emblems can transport our minds to Golgotha's hill. As we partake of this meal, we are expressing to the world that we believe God's Word and trust His grace.

> John 6:53: So, Jesus said to them, "truly, truly, I say to you, unless you eat the flesh of the Son of man, and drink his blood, you have no life in you."

ZEALOUS BUT WRONG

Hopefully, we have become familiar with the apostle Paul. We know he was a Roman citizen with much zeal persecuting Christians. Sadly, he thought he was doing a good thing. Paul was on his way to Damascus to arrest Christians when he had a close encounter with Jesus Christ. Paul found himself in a very difficult place after meeting Jesus. He suddenly knew his whole vocation was a terrible mistake. He may have felt his entire life had been wasted. He had some tough decisions to make—would he go back and face Christian families he had torn apart? We know he experienced sorrow and regret for what he had done.

I love Paul's question when he finally understood who Jesus really was. Paul said, "Lord, what do you want me to do?" (Acts 9:6).

Whether you are brokenhearted, broke, or wrapped up in this world, Jesus will meet you where you are. Around this table, we are up close and personal with our Savior. It is never too late for a fresh start.

> Luke 22:19 (NKJV): And he took bread, and when he had given thanks, he broke it and gave it to them, saying, "this is my body, which is given for you. Do this in remembrance of me."

The Best of His Love

I was traveling and listening to the radio. A song from the sixties came on called, "The Best of My Love." Even after the song was over, the title kept going through my mind. I started thinking about how God expresses His love. He gave us a beautiful creation to enjoy. He gives us, minute by minute, the air we breathe. He gives us food to sustain our bodies. He gives man dominion over animals. He created us in His image. He gives us mercy, grace, forgiveness, and hope. He gives Christians His Holy Spirit. We could write a book on the many ways God expresses His love to us. Providing we continue to abide in Christ, the Holy Spirit will continue to teach, convict, encourage, and comfort us—the gift that keeps on giving.

We celebrate the best of God's love as we meet around this table—the gift of God's one and only Son.

Romans 5:8 (NIV): But God shows his love for us in that while we were still sinners, Christ died for us.

ARE YOU FAMOUS?

young preacher had delivered a powerful, emotion-filled sermon, to which the congregation responded with loud amens; some people raised their arms, praising God. The preacher's seven-year-old daughter was quiet on the ride home. She was apparently thinking about what she had witnessed during the worship service. She was thinking about how excited the people seemed by her daddy's preaching.

Later, at the dinner table, she looked up at him and asked, "Daddy, are we famous?" He smiled at her and said, "No, of course we aren't famous." Libby thought for a minute and responded, "Well, we would be if more people knew about us."

I think that sometimes we put Jesus on the back burner in our daily lives. We focus attention on ourselves, and perhaps we want to be recognized for who and what we are for different reasons. Perhaps we are absorbed with our personal wants and plans that we can crowd Jesus out of the picture.

The apostle Paul told us in Philippians 3:8, "I also have considered every- thing to be loss in view of the surpassing value of knowing Christ Jesus, my Lord."

Our human nature leads us to desire respect, recognition, and value. There is one simple way to know just how much you are worth. Think of the ridicule, mocking, humiliation, and, finally, death on a cross. We don't need recognition or fame; we need only to be part of the family of God.

> Matthew 7:24 (CSB): Therefore, everyone who hears these words, and acts on them will be like a wise man, who built his house on the rock.

How's Your Foundation?

A young couple had inherited an old home that had been in the husband's family for generations. They began some renovations on the old house and wanted to convert the garage into an office. The contractor came to him with the news that he would need to demolish the entire garage and start over. It seemed that the walls had very little foundation. The owner started calculating the extra cost and asked the contractor if he could just patch it up. The builder was adamant and said, "Unless we go down the proper depth for the foundation, the building inspector won't approve it. The right foundation is vital to your home."

We know that in our Christian walk, we need to be building on the firm foundation. Part of this foundation is belief in His virgin birth, death, and resurrection and victory over death. We can't see the foundation; it may be hidden, but it is vitally important to the stability of our faith.

We are reminded throughout the New Testament to gather around the communion table; it is part of our foundation. When we participate in the bread and the cup, we are telling the world we are waiting His return.

John 3:16 (NAS): For God so loved the world that he gave his one and only son that whosoever believes on him, shall not perish, but have everlasting life.

JESUS LOVES

A minister was doing some premarital counseling. He asked the groom- to-be, "How do you know that you really love your fiancée?" It was a loaded question intended to help understand the young man's motives for the upcoming wedding. After a few thoughtful moments, he responded, "I know I love her because I want to spend the rest of my life making her happy." Scripture speaks of always seeking the best for others, rather than ourselves.

There are several Greek words for love. The highest form of love is agape love; it is defined and driven by self-sacrifice. There is always a price tag for agape or selfless love. We do for others first. Nowhere is it more evident than the event of Christ's crucifixion. The true measure of love is what you are willing to give up for it.

I love the lyrics from the song, "Amazing Love." It goes, "Amazing love, how can it be, that thou my God, should die for me?"

2 Corinthians 4:16-18 (NKJV): Therefore, outwardly we are wasting away, yet inwardly we are being renewed day by day.

BEING RENEWED

There is a field I pass every time I drive to church. An old tree stands in the middle of the field. It catches my eye each time I pass by. The tree is tall, and its branches are beautifully shaped. It looks almost majestic, and I think it would make a beautiful painting. It looks very healthy and stout.

After a terrible storm with high winds and heavy rain, I noticed that some of the tree's branches were beaten pretty bad. Once beautiful, now the branches lay all around on the ground. The tree had been through many windy and snowy storms over the years.

I am reminded of how we may look healthy and strong, just like the tree, but as life batters us with trials and troubles, we can get beaten down too. We may find ourselves emotionally and spiritually drained. However, the Word tells us to remain (or abide) in Christ, to remain faithful to Him so we will receive our reward of heaven. Storms will pass, but heaven is eternal.

There are good reasons we meet around this table. We do it because Jesus tells us to. We do it to follow the example Christ gave His apostles. We do it to draw near to the heart of God. We do it to remind ourselves of Christ's sacrifice. We do it to renew our minds and hearts.

John 3:16 (KJV): For God so loved the world, that whosever believeth on him, shall not perish, but have everlasting life.

LOVE DEFINED

The jewelry stores claim that if you love your wife, you will give her a diamond. Retailers promote heart-shaped boxes of chocolate to tell your spouse you love him or her. We must not forget the florist…or Hallmark. If you love someone, you should send him or her the best.

Scripture is truth; truth is found in 1 Corinthians 13. Love manifests itself by doing these things:

Love is patient, love is kind. It does not envy, it does not boast, it is not proud, it is not rude, it is not self-seeking, it is not easily angered, it keeps no records of wrongs. Love does not delight in evil, but rejoices with truth. It always trusts, always hopes, always perseveres. Love never fails.

If your life reveals these things to someone, then you are expressing a great love for him or her.

When we come around this communion table, we are responding to God's love as we remember the sacrifice of His one and only Son.

> 1 Corinthians 11:28-29 (NKJV): A man ought to examine himself before he eats of the bread and drinks of the cup. For anyone who eats and drinks without discerning the body of the Lord, eats and drinks judgement on himself.

CHECK-UP

Our daughter and son-in-law adopted twin boys when they were just one day old. These twins are now seven years old. They have made sure to take the boys for monthly and now yearly check-ups. Since we had no biological or medical history of the boys, it was more important to have the check-ups. You and I are also adopted, adopted and grafted into God's family. You and I know how crucial our check-ups are. We want to know if there is an illness or condition that needs to be treated.

We also need spiritual check-ups. Let us just say we attend church regularly, we read our Bible daily, we help those in need, and we pray often. We do a lot of things that are expected of us as Christians. But we can do a personal check-up each time we meet around the Lord's table.

The communion table is two-fold. It is a memorial service for Christ, and it is a celebration for us. We recognize His death, and we anticipate His return.

CHRISTMAS/NEW YEAR

L uke 2:35, 37: The angel replied to her: The Holy Spirit will come upon you, and the power of the Most High will overshadow you. Therefore the holy one to be born will be called the Son of God. For nothing will be impossible with God.

CANCEL CHRISTMAS

I overheard a conversation that started me thinking about how and why people celebrate Christmas as they do. The lady was telling her friend about the year that her family cancelled Christmas. It had been their tradition to travel north to Michigan and spend the holidays with the family. This one year when they cancelled Christmas, the weather was extremely bad for travel, and all airline flights to Michigan had been grounded because of ice and snow. So they cancelled Christmas until the next December.

Celebrating with family is enjoyable, and memories are made. However, we know that family gatherings aren't the real reason for the celebration. Christmas is about celebrating the birth of a King, a Redeemer, a Savior.

The holiday celebrations are subject to be postponed or cancelled—but the reason for the Christmas celebration will remain until the Lord comes the second time.

> 1 Corinthians 11:26 (KJV): For as often as you eat this bread, and drink this cup, you proclaim the Lord's death until he comes.

Mary, Did You Know?

Singer Mark Lowry wrote a song a few years ago that has become a classic. The lyrics of the song are so thought-provoking:

Mary, did you know that your baby boy would someday walk on water? Mary, did you know that your baby boy would save our sons and daughters? Did you know that your baby boy has come to make you new? This child that you delivered, would soon deliver you. Mary did you know that your baby boy would give sight to a blind man? Mary did you know that your baby boy would calm a storm with his hand? Did you know that your baby boy has walked where angels trod? And, when you kiss your baby boy, you've kissed the face of God.

A mother's influence on a child is an awesome responsibility. A mother nurtures, comforts, and teaches a child in her own personal way. A mother is a strong, influential part of her child's development and character. This makes me think of the pride Mary must have felt as she followed her Son and witnessed His healing and teaching. Afterward, the pain and anguish she must have felt as she watched the beatings and, ultimately, her Son's broken and bleeding body on that cross—a mother's broken heart.

We meet at this table to remember the Boy who became the Man who became our Savior.

Acts 2:42 (CSB): They devoted themselves to the apostles teaching, to the fellowship, to the breaking of bread and to prayer.

PATIENTLY WAIT

If patience isn't one of your gifts, then I feel the Christmas season can be especially difficult for you. I say that because this time of the year, we do a lot more waiting than doing. We wait in slow traffic, and we wait in long check-out lanes for our purchases. We wait for relatives to arrive. My hardest time of waiting is for the holidays meals to be done. As for the younger folks, and sometimes the adults too, there is the anxious wait for the opening of gifts.

If we can focus with our spiritual eyes during this season, we will recognize that Christmas is a time of waiting, waiting and experiencing something deeper and more intimate. It is a time of more important things than our family's holiday traditions. Just like the ancient Israelites and prophets of old who were waiting for their Messiah, we too are waiting for Jesus. He arrived as a babe in the manger, but now we wait for His second coming.

God also waits. He waits for people to see His glory. He waits for people to admit they are lost. He waits for people to say yes to the gift of His Son. God waits for man to repent and turn from sin. God is patiently waiting.

God made the first move when He came as a babe; His second move was when He became the sacrifice for our sins, and His third move will be His return for His children.

John 14:6 (CSB): I am the way, the truth and the life. No one come to the Father, except through me. If you know me, you will also know my Father.

TIME TO CELEBRATE

I recall the chorus from a song we sang in the Christmas cantata years ago. It goes like this, "Celebrations come because of something good— celebrations we love to recall—Mary had a baby born in Bethlehem—the greatest celebration of them all."

We celebrate Christmas to recognize the birth of Christ. We celebrate when something good happens to us.

Yes, Mary gave the world a gift, the Son of God. Thirty-three years later, God gave us the same Son again as a gift for our salvation.

We celebrate Christ's birth once a year. But we celebrate His death and His resurrection each time we meet around this communion table.

> Philippians 2:7-8 (CSB): Being found in appearance as a man, He humbled Himself by becoming obedient to the point of death, even death on a cross.

WRAPPED

At our house, when our kids and now our grandkids attack the gifts under the tree, I follow close behind, gathering the boxes and bows that I can re- use next year. All that hard work from several weeks of wrapping gifts is scattered across the floor. The presentation and wrapping of the gifts are part of the beauty of the gift.

It makes me think of the wrapping of Christ when He came into the world. He could have come to earth in a blazing, mind-boggling show of power, lighting up the sky with His glory. Just the opposite—Scripture tells us He chose to wrap Himself in the likeness of men.

Why is the wrapping so important? In God's infinite wisdom, He chose to be wrapped in human-ness so, being like man, He would experience the struggles of mankind. He experienced deep loneliness, betrayal, and public shame. He was misunderstood and falsely accused. He understood firsthand the pains of human life.

So, when you think of Jesus as our gift this Christmas, keep the wrapping in mind and know He understands you.

A Holy Savior wrapped in the likeness of man.

> 2 Corinthians 5:17 (ESV): Therefore, if anyone is in Christ, he is a new creation, the old has passed away, behold, the new has come.

NEW BEGINNING

This is a new year, a new week, and a new beginning.

What is your resolution? We have plenty of things to think about in making ourselves better people. A few to mention—take better care of our health, study Scripture more, pray more, practice more patience, change some bad habits, and become bolder in our witness. Whatever we need to change, whether physical, mental, or spiritual, this is a great place to start.

Christ came into this world to save us, and He also gave us His Holy Spirit to teach, convict, comfort, and renew us. Paul told us in the book of Romans that Christ died for us while we were sinners. We aren't deserving of God's grace.

We remain faithful around this table because Jesus said to do this in remembrance of Him.

1 Corinthians 11:26 (CSB): For as often as you eat this bread and drink this cup, you proclaim the Lord's death until he comes.

BESTSELLER

There are countless self-improvement books available for us to purchase. Beginning with each new year, we usually make a list of things we hope to improve about ourselves.

We don't really have to wait till New Year's arrives to begin any type of self-improvement. We can begin at any time. As a matter of fact, the ultimate bestseller for self-improvement is your Bible. James, Jesus's brother, told us to look into the Word to see ourselves as we are and to show us where we need to be.

Each time we meet around this table, we meet with the Man who can make us whole. We meet to remember His sacrifice and to pledge our commitment to this covenant He made with us. **As** we do this, His Spirit renews us.

> Romans 8:35 (CSB): Christ Jesus is the one who died, but even more, has been raised, he also is at the right hand of God, and intercedes for us.

364 Days

After celebrating the Christmas season, recognizing the birth of our Savior, I am questioning something. How does the world celebrate Jesus Christ the other 364 days of the year? How do we celebrate and discern the Jesus that lived for thirty-three years? Is Jesus still here?

We read in Scripture that we have security if we are abiding in Christ. Not that we won't have trials and troubles, but that our souls are safe in Christ. Paul assured us that we are safe, secure, and victorious in Christ's great love. We are more than conquerors through Christ.

We continue to celebrate Christ through our communion service. Jesus said that as often as we do this, we are showing His death until He returns. Amen, what a Savior.

When all around me is darkness
And earthly joys have flown, My
 Savior whispers His promise Never
to leave me alone.

Acknowledgement

My heart is filled with love for my husband, who has provided for our family for over four decades. He not only provides, he perseveres, and he inspires me with his faith and insight into Scripture. He and I have worked as a team for thirty years in our home congregations of The Church of Christ—myself as a teacher, and he as a deacon, elder, and teacher.

The Lord is our rock and salvation.

www.ingramcontent.com/pod-product-compliance
Lightning Source LLC
Chambersburg PA
CBHW051236120626
46547CB00013B/1676